GLUTEN-FREE DIARY-FREE DESSERT COOKBOOK

50 DELICIOUS, FAMILY-FRIENDLY

DESSERT RECIPES

SHIOBAN CRUW

TABLE OF CONTENTS

Introduction

More and more people are "going gluten-free" than ever before, and with good reason. There is an enormous array of books and websites that can explain the benefits of a gluten-free diet, whether you have a serious wheat allergy or not.

All recipes are written to feed a family of four – however, that will vary due to the appetites of your loved ones and the size of your kids (if you have any)! I believe in flexibility in the kitchen, so experiment as you like, adding a little more sauce here, a little less cheese there. The photos show a typical single serving, but as always, suit to your needs. Often, amounts of spices, garnishes, and/or veggies are not given. Use according to your preference.

This book is dedicated to those people who cannot go by without a single day without those specific foods. The book compiles not only breakfast, lunch, dinner, snacks and dessert recipes for gluten intolerant people but it also opens up options for lunches and dinners as well. The recipes are full of variations.

Chapter 1: Introduction to the Gluten-Free Diet

What is gluten?

Gluten, a family of protein, is found in grains like ryes, wheat, and spelt are gluten-containing grains. Gluten is responsible for forming a sticky network or adding a glue-like consistency in the foods like in dough for loaves of bread, cookies, etc. Gluten adds elasticity into the dough, gives the bread to rise when baked, and delivers it a satisfying texture.

Gluten is made up of two main proteins that are gliadin and glutenin. Among these two proteins, glutenin has most of the adverse effects on health. Although most of the people are gluten tolerant but it can cause harmful effects for the people with certain conditions, which includes people suffering from gluten sensitivity, celiac diseases, wheat allergies, etc.

The most common symptom of gluten intolerance is digestion discomfort. There could be other reasons for this discomfort as well. If you think you have digestive comfort, ask your doctor to check you for celiac disease first. If the test comes out positive, consult your doctor first before trying the gluten-free diet. But, if you don't have celiac diseases, the best way to figure out if you are gluten intolerance is through strictly follow a gluten-free diet for few weeks. Then introduce the gluten back into your diet and see if its symptoms are improving or not.

Gluten is primarily found in foods like bread, pasta, cakes, muffins, crackers, and pizza dough. Wheat, barley, and rye are used in many baked goods because the gluten in these grains provides excellent elasticity, structure, and texture. Gluten is what causes pizza to have a chewy, stretchy texture. It gives French bread its soft white center and chewy crust. Gluten makes cinnamon rolls stretchy, soft, and light. It helps give structure to bread dough when rising, so that the bread becomes tall and stays tall after baking and cooling.

Avoiding gluten in your children's diets can be difficult for several reasons. The biggest reason is that ingredients containing gluten are not required by law to be listed on food labels. However, by law, the top eight food allergens must be listed on every food label in the United States, and wheat (which is a primary source of gluten) is one of them. So although you may not see "gluten" in the ingredients list, you can look for food allergen information, for example, "contains wheat."

The real deal on celiac disease and gluten sensitivity

Celiac disease (also known as celiac sprue or gluten-sensitive enteropathy) is an auto-immune and digestive disorder that occurs in about one in 100 people in the United States. For children with this disorder, gluten can cause serious damage to their intestine if it is ingested. If your child has celiac disease or gluten sensitivity, gluten damages the "villi" in their intestines. Since the villi (finger-like projections that contain most of the enzymes needed for digestion) are damaged for those with celiac disease, their bodies have enormous difficulty ingesting the healthy nutrients their bodies need such as fat, calcium, iron, and folate. It is a condition that causes many digestive symptoms due to difficulty in digestion of gluten. Those with celiac disease must avoid gluten-containing foods 100% of the time. Certain foods, such as oats, that do not contain gluten should be used carefully due to cross contamination that can occur while growing in fields near wheat or during processing on the same machines.

Some of the symptoms of celiac disease and gluten sensitivity include:

- Digestive problems such as bloating, vomiting, excess gas and/or pain, severe and/or chronic diarrhea, irritable bowel, weight loss, weight gain, etc.
- Constant and/or severe headaches or migraines
- Low levels of iron (anemia)
- Skin rashes (also known as dermatitis herpetiformis)
- Bone or joint pain
- Depression and/or anxiety
- Seizures
- Unexplained fatigue
- Failure to thrive

Most children have a healthy immune system that prevents the body from being harmed by gluten, but for those with celiac disease the only effective treatment is avoiding foods with gluten altogether.

To get your child tested for celiac disease and/or gluten sensitivity you need to visit your family doctor or a gastroenterologist, who will do a blood test to check for high levels of certain types of antibodies. If his blood test comes back with positive results for celiac disease, the doctor may then choose to do a biopsy of his small intestine to check for damage to the villi. A diagnosis is usually given using a combination of these diagnostic tests.

What foods contains gluten?

Starting with a gluten-free diet can be challenging at the start. You will have to shift on eating whole foods as they are naturally gluten-free. Along with the changes in the diet, you will have to start reading food labels on everything you are purchasing in the grocery store or when eating out. The following foods are the most common sources of gluten.

- Grains
- Wheat
- Rye
- Spelt
- Bread
- Pasta
- Cereal
- Crackers
- Cake
- Cookies
- Pastries
- All sort of wheat-based baked foods
- Fruits and Vegetables
- Canned vegetables and fruits
- Frozen vegetables and fruits
- Dried fruits
- Pre-chopped vegetables and fruits
- Proteins
- Processed meals like bacon, salami, pepperoni and hot dogs
- Cold cuts meats
- Breaded meat, fish or poultry
- Seitan
- Dairy Products
- Flavored milks
- Flavored yogurts
- Processed cheese product
- Cheese sauces
- Spreads
- Malted milk drinks
- Fats and Oils
- Cooking sprays

- Oils with added spices and flavors
- Beverages
- Premade smoothies
- All beverages with added flavoring
- Distilled liquor
- Vodka
- Whiskey
- Gin
- Sauces and condiments
- Wheat-based soy sauce
- Wheat-based teriyaki sauce
- Malt vinegar

The gluten-free diet for weight loss

Apart from people suffering from celiac diseases, many people have started following a gluten-free diet for dropping extra pounds of weight. And, the results have been magical. So instead of eating carefully, doing plenty of exercises, take a diet devoid of gluten and wheat. Here are some strategies to lose weight when you are on a gluten-free diet.

Avoid processed gluten-free foods
You will need to steer clear from wheat and gluten-free processed foods. There are some grain-free gluten-free products like gluten-free cake mixes, snacks, cookies, pizza, and bread, but they actually have higher calories than their wheat-based versions. So, don't take the label of gluten-free food products as "calorie-free."

Count your calories
Just like you used to count calories on the non-gluten-free diet, you have keep continuing this when you go gluten-free. You will find drop in your weight effortlessly as gluten-free diet curb the cravings and appetite. As a result, you eat fewer calories. However, you need to keep check on your calorie intake to keep your weight loss ball rolling.

Eat low-carb or Paleo also
Along with cutting the carbs and gluten from the wheat, giving up every high-carb food is best for weight loss on a gluten-free diet. However, make sure you are still consuming fiber, valuable vitamins, and other nutrients as well to meet your dietary requirements.

Don't forget to exercise
Exercise is the most important tip of all for losing weight on a gluten-free diet. Eliminating the gluten and wheat may help in losing weight more quickly, but if you want to speed things up, you are going to need to break a sweat. Hitting the gym and doing exercise can help in losing even more fat. So, along with following the gluten-free diet to the T, you need to make some time for some healthy physical activities as well.

What Is A Gluten Free Diet?

Gluten is a find of protein that can be detected in elements like barley, wheat, rye, and triticale. Gluten is usually found when starch is extracted from any cereal grain. Therefore, the substance is rather primal in our everyday meals. But certain people with celiac diseases cannot consume gluten due to their health issues as the doctors and nutritionists put it, they produce inflammation in small intestines. Gluten-free eating helps one with celiac disease to keep the balance of his body and evade unwanted complications.

Gluten free diet is not only directed towards the people who are affected by celiac disease, some people have the condition of "non-celiac gluten sensitivity" hence the diet helps those as well to keep them healthy.

But as the alarming fact already been established that eating gluten is in our everyday menu and without it there are hardly few options left to go to! For instance, the ingredient "flour" is almost in every recipe, it is in our breakfast food, no one can imagine of making delicious appetizers without flour. Flour is in our desserts and it can also be found in our main course! And the most crucial part is the "baking", how can one bake muffins, cakes, pizza etc. without flour?

When all these terrible but valid questions hover around the head, it becomes rather difficult to switch to this beneficial diet as one may find themselves giving up a lot of the delicious food items. Well, initially every little endeavor takes a huge load on ones chest, but slowly with the passage of time if proper resources are available and one is determine enough, the transformation becomes much easier.

The key to this transformation is:

- Take baby steps
- Do not be too rigid right at the beginning
- Look for potential substitutes
- Ask people who are already in the diet

- Be creative and open minded
- Try new recipes
- Read a lot of gluten-free diet books
- Look at the positives
- Try to overlook the negatives

It is a diet completely free of all foods derived from these gluten grains. Unfortunately, gluten shows up unexpectedly in many processed foods that contain food additives, flavorings, stabilizers, or thickening agents.

What grain foods and starches are acceptable on a gluten-free diet?

There are many grains to choose from, but most are not common or always readily available. Because gluten is the protein that helps bread to rise, breads made without gluten have a different texture. They also can be quite costly.

The most common gluten-free starchy foods include corn, potatoes, and rice, but there are other non-gluten whole grains that are more nutritious. Some, such as quinoa, are not actually grains but are treated as such because they are satisfying and taste like grains.

Other less common grains and starches to try on a gluten-free diet include: millet, sorghum, tapioca, arrowroot, teff, amaranth, buckwheat. Even bean and nut flours may be used in gluten-free baking! Some examples include garbanzo bean flour, soy flour, chestnut flour, coconut flour, hazelnut or almond meal, or chia seed. These tend to be higher in protein and dietary fiber than wheat flour. When buying products made from these flours, it is important to be careful of other possible sources of gluten. For example, pastas that contain buckwheat or amaranth also may contain wheat flour.

Food that you must avoid:
- Barley
- Rye
- Wheat
- Graham flour
- Triticale
- Farina
- Pastas
- Kamut
- Durum flour
- Semolina

- Spelt
- Breads
- Seasoned snack foods, such as potato and tortilla chips
- Beer
- Sauces, including soy sauce
- Candies
- French fries
- Cakes and pies
- Cereals
- Vegetables in sauce
- Self-basting poultry
- Gravies
- Cookies and crackers
- Soups and soup bases
- Imitation meat or seafood
- Croutons
- Communion wafers
- Matzo
- Processed luncheon meats
- Salad dressings
- Seasoned rice mixes

Gluten-free for beginners

If you're already familiar with living gluten-free you may skip this section and go right into the healthy gluten-free recipes. However, if you are new to the gluten-free lifestyle, you may find this section to be quite useful.

Gluten-free Shopping You're advised to go shopping before you start your exciting gluten-free lifestyle. Preparation is essentially worth the effort and will make things so much easier. This will avoid you winding up in a frustrating situation where you are left with little or no options. Besides, lack of planning is the main reason for failures in life.

Choosing your Food Whenever you go gluten-free shopping you should ensure that you buy antibiotic-free and hormone-free animal, poultry, fish and red meat. You should look for free-range poultry and eggs as well as grass-fed beef, organic pork, wild fish or grass-fed butter. It is also important to choose freshly frozen meat which is also referred to as "flash" frozen.

Essential Gluten-free Kitchen Tools

There are several essential tools that could make your gluten-free lifestyle much easier. Though not all of these items are needed for the recipes in this book, they are simply essential items that you'll find useful in your gluten-free kitchen.

Apart from your slow cooker, here is a list of some other common essential gluten-free kitchen tools:

- A food processor
- A ladle
- A colander
- Ziplock storage bags of different sizes
- A powerful blender
- A dutch oven
- grill pans
- A set of good-quality knives
- Wooden cutting boards—use separate boards for animal products and fruits or vegetables
- An 8-inch nonstick sauté pan
- A 12-inch nonstick sauté pan (avoid nonstick pans with Teflon or other health risks due to poorer quality)
- An 8-quart stockpot
- Cooling rack
- 3 or 4 cookie or baking sheets
- Oven mittens
- Storage glass jars for condiments
- Natural parchment paper
- A lemon/citrus reamer
- A food mill/potato ricer
- A 2-quart saucepan with lid
- A 4-quart saucepan with lid
- A foil lined baking tray
- A coffee grinder for flaxseed or similar stuff
- Wire whisks
- Spring tongs
- Rubber spatulas
- Assorted measuring cups and spoons (1 quart, pint, 1 cup etc.) dry and liquid style
- A food scale
- Muffin pans
- Baking pans
- Skewers
- An instant-read chef 's thermometer
- Timer

- Mixing bowls of different sizes
- Electric mixer
- Consider that this is not a conclusive list. Besides, you may already have some of these items in your kitchen.

Planning for a gluten-free lifestyle

If your child has been diagnosed with celiac disease, the first thing you will want to do is gather all the information you can. Ask your pediatrician to recommend a nutritionist or registered dietitian who can give you a better understanding of what going gluten-free really means. A nutritionist may also request that your doctor order tests to help you discover if your child has any additional food sensitivities or nutritional deficiencies. These tests may include a bone scan or tests of vitamin D, calcium, iron, zinc, B12, folate, or thyroid levels. Once the doctor and nutritionist have a better picture of what's going on in your child's body, they can help determine the best plan of action and what gluten-free foods will be the most nutritious choices.

Research online
Do some online research to find local grocery stores that have gluten-free foods, along with local restaurants with gluten-free items on their menus. There are countless websites available that can help you find local gluten-free resources such as community support groups, books to help educate yourself and your family, gluten-free recipes and menus, and even gluten-free shopping guides. Your community may even have a gluten-free bakery that offers baked goods like pizza, sandwich bread, cakes, and cookies.

Stay Safe While Dining Out
Every time you visit a restaurant with your child make sure to assess the knowledge of the wait staff and kitchen staff. Ask your server for a gluten-free menu. Ask about the steps taken in the kitchen area to prevent cross-contamination. If a waiter or chef doesn't understand what gluten-free means, it may be a sign that gluten-free options are not available. Never be afraid to ask specific questions—your child's health is important!

The Benefits of Gluten Free Eating

Gluten Free Diet will help you restore your body's ability to absorb optimum nutrients from your food. And since the diet itself should consist of healthy whole foods, you will have no trouble at all getting all the much-needed vitamins, minerals and other nutrients that your cells need. Once your body starts to get fully nourished, you will then be able to experience all the wonderful benefits of Gluten Free eating. Here are the most commonly noted benefits:

No More Allergy-Related Problems

If your intolerance to gluten has been causing you diarrhea, constipation, heartburn, acid reflux, bloating and other allergy related symptoms, then the diet will certainly eliminate those. Some who are severely allergic to gluten have even reported that they no longer have acne, rosacea, canker sores, lactose intolerance, and – in women – abnormal menstrual cycles a few weeks after following the diet. The relief that you will finally get is definitely well worth giving up gluten!

Better Energy Levels

Great energy that lasts throughout the day can only be possible in the healthy way if you eat nourishing food. No longer will you experience headaches, fatigue, sluggishness, low mood, and the inability to concentrate when on the Gluten Free Diet.

You Become More Health-Conscious

Those who follow the Gluten Free Diet develop good eating habits because of the simple fact that they need to choose their food carefully. They are also more conscious about the effects of eating unhealthy food. Thus, they are able to manage their weight more easily and manage their blood sugar and cholesterol levels more effectively.

Overall, your number one priority when it comes to this diet should be to heal your body and improve your health. If the body is healthy, it will naturally reflect through your appearance and performance. You will be able to work productively because your mind is sharp, and your body is strong. Your skin will become clear, glowing and supple, and your hair and nails strong. You will be a lot more resistant to illness because your body is no longer stressed from the symptoms caused by gluten. All these effects and more will make your life so much more enjoyable and fulfilling.

Chapter 2: Dessert and snacks

Chocolate Muffins

Preparation Time: 10 minutes
Cooking Time: 20 minutes
Servings: 4

Ingredients:

2 1/2 cups gluten free flour

1 cup brown sugar

1 tbsp white vinegar

1/2 cup cocoa powder

1/2 tsp bicarbonate of soda

1 cup almond milk

125g almond butter, melted

1 tsp vanilla extract

Chocolate icing:

125g almond butter, chopped

200g dark chocolate, chopped

1/2 cup icing sugar mixture

Directions:

Preheat the oven to 400F.

Grease the muffin tray and set aside for now.

In a bowl combine the cocoa powder with the flour and add bicarbonate of soda to it.

Then pour in the almond milk, vanilla, almond butter and vinegar to it.

Mix well and then pour into the muffin tray.

Bake for only 20 minutes.

For the icing, in an ovenproof bowl add the chocolate with almond butter and microwave for 30 sec.

Give it a stir and again microwave it, see if it has melt, if not then repeat again.

Take off the oven and let it cool.

 Now spread over the muffins and serve.

Chocolate Almond Bark

Preparation time: 10 minutes
Cooking time: 20 minutes
Servings: 4

Ingredients:

1 3/4 cup cacao

1/4 cup slivered almonds, unsalted

1 tablespoon erythritol sweetener

1/4 cup almond butter, unsweetened

Directions

Place cacao in a heatproof bowl, add butter and sweetener and microwave for 1 to 2 minutes until cacao and butter have melted, stirring every 30 seconds.

Take a baking sheet, line it with parchment sheet, then pour the cacao mixture on it and spread it evenly with the back of a spoon.

Sprinkle almond on top of cacao mixture and then freeze for 1 Minute until hard.

Then break it into pieces, place the pieces in a large plastic bag, and store in the freezer for up to three months.

Lime and Avocado Tart

Preparation time: 4 minutes
Cooking time: 10 minutes
Servings: 8

Ingredients:
For the Crust:

1/4 cup shredded coconut, unsweetened

1/2 cup chopped pecans

1/2 cup chopped dates

2 teaspoons lime zest

1/8 teaspoon sea salt

For the Tart Filling:

1 1/2 cups avocado puree

1/4 cup lime juice

1/4 cup honey

1 tablespoon coconut oil

1 teaspoon lime zest

Directions

Prepare the crust, and for this, place all its ingredients in a food processor and pulse until a sticky paste comes together.

Spoon the mixture evenly between two mini springform pans, spread and press it evenly and then freeze for 30 minutes.

Meanwhile, prepare the filling, and for this, place all its ingredients in a blender and pulse until creamy.

Take out the frozen crusts from the freezer, pour half of the filling in one pan and the other half of filling in the second pan, smooth the top, and continue freezing for a minimum of 2 Minutes.

Then wrap each tart in plastic wrap and freeze for up to three months.

When ready to eat, let the tart sit at room temperature for 15 minutes, then cut it into slices and serve.

Brownies

Preparation time: 5 minutes
Cooking time: 20 minutes
Servings: 8

Ingredients:

1 cup vanilla almonds, honey roasted

2 tablespoons cocoa powder

20 Medjool dates, pitted

1 tablespoon water

Directions

Place the almonds in a food processor, pulse until coarsely chopped, tip the almonds into a bowl and then set aside until required.

Add dates in the food processor, pulse until coarsely chopped, add cocoa powder and water, and pulse again until the dough comes together.

Add almonds, pulse again until incorporated, then transfer the dough in a large bowl and knead for 3 minutes until smooth.

Place a large piece of parchment paper on a clean working space, place dough on it, and roll it into 1/3-inch thick slab.

Use a knife to cut squares from the dough, about eight, and wrap each brownie in plastic wrap and store in the freezer for up to three months.

Vanilla and Honey Bananas

Servings: 4

Preparation time: 10 minutes
Cooking time: 10 Minute

Ingredients:
5 bananas, sliced

1 teaspoon vanilla extract

1 tablespoon honey

5 tablespoons brown sugar

½ cup condensed milk

½ cup evaporated milk

½ cup milk powder

Chocolate syrup

Directions:

In a slow cooker, gently mix sliced bananas, vanilla extract, honey, brown sugar, condensed milk, evaporated milk and milk powder.

Cook for 1 Minute on a low setting.

Serve with chocolate syrup.

Cinnamon Pears

Servings: 4

Preparation time: 10 minutes
Cooking time: 20 Minutes

Ingredients:
5 pears, sliced into two

2 teaspoons of cinnamon

1 teaspoon nutmeg

2 tablespoons honey

4 tablespoons brown sugar

Directions:

In a slow cooker, combine the pears, cinnamon, nutmeg, honey, and brown sugar.

Cook for 2 Minutes on high heat.

Sprinkle with more cinnamon before serving.

Baked Tortilla Chips

Preparation time: 10 minutes
Cooking time: 20 minutes
Servings: 4

Ingredients

5 corn tortillas

Canola oil

Sea salt

Directions:

Preheat oven to 350ºF.

Cut tortillas into 8 wedges each.

Spread oil on cookie sheet with a brush.

Spread tortilla wedges on cookie sheet in a single layer.

Brush tops of tortilla wedges with oil and sprinkle with salt.

Bake 13–15 minutes, until golden and crispy.

Easy Gravy

Preparation time: 10 minutes
Cooking time: 20 minutes
Servings: 4

Ingredients

1 gluten-free bouillon cube (vegetable, chicken, or beef) 1 cup plus 2 tablespoons water

1/4 teaspoon poultry seasoning 1/4 teaspoon sea salt 1/4 teaspoon freshly ground black pepper 1 tablespoon cornstarch

Directions:

Dissolve bouillon cube in 1 cup boiling water.

Add poultry seasoning, salt, and pepper to bouillon.

In a separate small bowl, thoroughly combine cornstarch with 2 tablespoons cold water.

Add diluted cornstarch to other mixture, stirring for several minutes until combined and thickened. Store in an airtight container in the refrigerator for up to 1 week.

Hummus

Preparation time: 10 minutes
Cooking time: 20 minutes
Servings: 4

Ingredients

2 cups cooked garbanzo beans (homemade or canned)

2 teaspoons lemon juice

2 tablespoons tahini (sesame seed paste)

3 tablespoons olive oil

1 clove garlic

1/4 teaspoon cumin 1/8 teaspoon salt

Directions:

If using canned garbanzo beans, drain and rinse beans.

Combine all ingredients in a food processor or blender.

Process until smooth. Serve as a dip or sandwich spread. Store in an airtight container in the refrigerator for up to 1 week.

Hummus Yogurt Dipping Sauce

Preparation time: 10 minutes
Cooking time: 20 minutes
Servings: 4

Ingredients

1 (15-ounce) can garbanzo beans

1–2 cloves crushed garlic

1 tablespoon lemon juice

1/2 cup plus 1 tablespoon plain yogurt or nondairy alternative such as So Delicious Coconut Milk Yogurt 1 teaspoon sea salt

1/2 teaspoon cumin

Directions:

Drain can of beans and save liquid.

In a food processor, combine all ingredients and blend well.

Use liquid from garbanzo beans to thin hummus to desired consistency. Store in an airtight container in the refrigerator for up to 1 week.

Pineapple Salsa

Preparation time: 10 minutes
Cooking time: 20 minutes
Servings: 4

Ingredients

1 cup diced fresh pineapple

1/2 cup red pepper, diced 1/2 cup yellow pepper, diced 1/2 cup black beans, drained and rinsed 1/4 cup red onion, diced 1/4 cup cilantro, finely chopped 1/4 cup orange-pineapple juice 2 tablespoons lime juice

Salt and pepper to taste

Directions:

In large bowl, combine pineapple, red pepper, yellow pepper, black beans, onion, and cilantro and mix well.

In small bowl, combine orange-pineapple juice and lime juice. Pour into large bowl.

Mix all ingredients together; season with salt and pepper to taste. Store in an airtight container in the refrigerator for up to 1 week.

Refried Pinto Beans

Preparation time: 10 minutes
Cooking time: 20 minutes
Servings: 4

Ingredients

1 cup dried pinto beans (or 1 [15-ounce] can)

1 tablespoon olive oil

1/2 onion, finely chopped 1 clove garlic, minced

1 teaspoon cumin

Directions:

If using dried beans, soak 6–8 Minutes or overnight before cooking.

Drain soaking water from beans, rinse, and combine beans with 3–4 cups water. Bring to a simmer with lid tilted.

Cook 1–11/2 Minutes or until tender.

Drain and rinse either cooked beans or canned beans if using.

In a medium saucepan or sauté pan, heat olive oil over medium heat.

Add onion and garlic.

Cook until onion is tender, 3–5 minutes.

Add beans and cumin and heat through.

Remove from heat and mash with a potato masher or fork. Store in an airtight container in the refrigerator for up to 1 week.

Creamy Salsa Dip

Preparation time: 10 minutes
Cooking time: 20 minutes
Servings: 4

Ingredients

1 tablespoon mayonnaise

1 tablespoon mild salsa

1/2 teaspoon honey

Combine all ingredients.

Directions:

Stir thoroughly. Store in an airtight container in the refrigerator for up to 1 week.

Sweet Sunflower-Seed Butter Dip

Preparation time: 10 minutes
Cooking time: 20 minutes
Servings: 4

Ingredients

1 tablespoon vanilla yogurt or nondairy alternative such as So
Delicious Coconut Milk Yogurt 1 tablespoon sunflower-seed butter

1 teaspoon honey

Directions:

Combine all ingredients in a small bowl.

Stir well and serve.

Tropical Pudding Pie Dip

Preparation time: 10 minutes
Cooking time: 20 minutes
Servings: 4

Ingredients

1 small package gluten-free instant vanilla pudding

11/2 cups milk or nondairy alternative such as almond milk 1 cup vanilla yogurt or nondairy alternative such as So Delicious Coconut Milk Yogurt 1/3 cup orange-pineapple juice 1/2 teaspoon orange or lemon zest

Directions:

Combine vanilla pudding and milk with a beater.

Once blended well, add remaining ingredients and blend until smooth.

Chill and serve. Store in an airtight container in the refrigerator for up to 1 week.

Spiced Up Veggies with Apples

Preparation time: 5 minutes
Cooking time: 6 Minutes

Servings: 8-10

Ingredients:
5 cups cabbage, shredded

½ cup onion, diced

4 cups of apples, diced

2 teaspoons chili powder

2 tablespoons honey

3 tablespoons brown sugar

1 teaspoon cinnamon

1 teaspoon black pepper, ground 4 tablespoons balsamic vinegar

Salt and pepper

Directions:

In a slow cooker, combine cabbage, onion, apples, chili powder, honey, brown sugar, cinnamon, black pepper, and balsamic vinegar.

Cook for 6 Minutes on a low setting.

Season with salt and pepper before serving.

Strawberry Fudge Slices

Preparation time: 25 minutes
Cooking time: 3 Minutes

Servings: 6

Ingredients:
2 cups strawberries, hulled and quartered ¼ cup brown sugar

2 tablespoons honey

1 cup of milk chocolate, melted 4 tablespoons butter, melted

2 teaspoons gluten-free cornstarch

Directions:

Place at the bottom of the slow cooker the melted butter, then the corn starch, then the milk chocolate.

Cook for 1 Minute on a high setting.

Add in the strawberries, honey, and brown sugar.

Cook for 2 Minutes on a high setting.

Cool until set. Slice into desired sizes before serving.

Chocolate Salted Caramel Mud Cakes

Preparation Time: 20 minutes
Cooking Time: 10 minutes
Servings: 2

Ingredients:

1/2 cup biscuit gluten free flour

1/3 cup cocoa powder, sifted

1 1/2 tbsp vegetable oil

6 jersey caramels, quartered

1 tsp arrowroot

1/2 cup caster sugar

1/2 cup almond milk

1 tsp salt

Vegan friendly Double cream, to serve

Directions:

Combine the flour with sugar, cocoa, almond milk, oil, and arrowroot together into a bowl.

Divide the milk into 4 portions into microwave protected bowls.

Now microwave for 1 minute and then add a little salt and half of the caramel on each bowl.

Then again microwave for a minute and add a little salt and the rest of the caramel and microwave for further 2 minutes.

Serve with vegan friendly cream.

Mexican Chocolate Cake

Preparation Time: 10 minutes
Cooking Time: 15 minutes
Servings: 4-6

Ingredients:
Dry

1 3/4 cups all-purpose glutenfree flour

3/4 cup coconut flour

1 1/2 cups raw cacao powder, sifted

1 tbsp baking soda

1 1/2 tsp Himalayan pink salt

3/4 tsp ground cinnamon

1/4 tsp cayenne pepper

Wet

1/2 cup extra virgin coconut oil

1/2 cup apple sauce

1 1/2 cups water

2 cups coconut nectar

2 tbsp orange zest

1 banana mashed

1 tbsp coconut oil

Frosting

1 cup raw cacao powder, sifted

1/4 cup orange juice

1/2 cup coconut nectar

1 tbsp orange zest

1/4 tsp cayenne powder

Pinch Himalayan pink salt

2 tbsp orange zest, to serve

1/2 cup slivered almonds, to serve

Directions:

Preheat the oven to 400F.

Grease a cake tin and line up baking paper to it.

In a mixing bowl combine all the dry ingredients together.

In another bowl combine all the wet ingredients together.

Now make a well into the dry ingredients and pour in the wet ingredients to it.

Make a smooth batter and then pour into the pre-greased cake tin.

Bake for about 45 minutes onto the preheated oven.

In a bowl combine all the frosting ingredients and pour over the cake when it has cooled down. Garnish with orange zest and almonds.

Fennel and Kale Smoothie

Preparation time: 5 min

Servings: 2

Ingredients:

1-2 ice cubes

1 cup coconut water

1 cup fennel

2-3 kale leaves

2-3 fresh figs

2 limes, juiced

Directions:

Combine ingredients in a blender and purée until smooth. Enjoy!

Kids' Favorite Kale Smoothie

Preparation time: 5 min

Servings: 2

Ingredients:

2-3 ice cubes

1½ cup apple juice

1 small apple, cut

½ cup pineapple chunks

½ cucumber, cut

3 leaves kale

Directions:

Combine ingredients in a blender and purée until smooth. Enjoy!

Kids' Favorite Spinach Smoothie

Preparation time: 5 min

Servings: 2

Ingredients:

1 frozen banana

1 cup orange juice

1 apple, cut

1 cup baby spinach

1 tsp vanilla extract

Directions:

Combine ingredients in a blender and purée until smooth. Enjoy!

Paleo Mojito Smoothie

Preparation time: 5 min

Servings: 2

Ingredients:

1 cup ice

1 cup coconut water, milk or plain water

1 big pear, chopped

2-3 limes, juiced, or peeled and cut

20-25 leaves fresh mint

3 dates, pitted

Directions:

Juice the limes or peel and cut them and combine with the other ingredients in a blender. Process until smooth. Enjoy!

Winter Greens Smoothie

Preparation time: 5 min

Servings: 2

Ingredients:

2 broccoli florets, frozen

1½ cup coconut water

½ banana

½ cup pineapple

1 cup fresh spinach

2 kale leaves

Directions:

Combine ingredients in blender and blend until smooth. Enjoy!

Hippie Protein Muffins

Preparation time: 5 minutes

Cooking Time: 20 minutes

Servings: 2

Ingredients

2 tablespoons coconut flour

2 tablespoons rice protein powder

1 tablespoons hemp seeds

2 tablespoons ground chia seeds

1 tablespoons flax seed meal

½ teaspoon baking powder

¼ teaspoon baking soda

½ cup unsweetened vanilla almond milk

½ -1 teaspoon granulated stevia or coconut sugar

Extra toppings-hemp seeds and chia seeds

Slightly melted coconut butter for topping

Directions

Preheat the oven to 350F. Grease the ramekins and keep aside.

In a mixing bowl, and put in coconut flour, protein powder, hemp seeds, flaxseeds, chia seeds, baking powder, baking soda and stevia. Pour almond milk and mix until smooth with no lumps.

Pour into the greased ramekins and bake for 20 minutes. Allow to cool completely before taking out and then top with coconut butter and seeds and serve.

Cinnamon Rolls

Preparation time: 10 minutes

Cooking Time: 5 minutes

Servings: 16 rolls

Ingredients

2 ½ cups of arrowroot powder or tapioca powder

3 cups of blanched almond flour

½ teaspoon salt

1 teaspoon grain free baking powder

3 teaspoon pectin

4 tablespoon refined coconut oil or dairy free melted butter

1 teaspoon distilled white vinegar

½ cup + 1 tablespoon almond milk

2 whole eggs

1 teaspoon vanilla

¼ cup honey

Filling

2 tablespoon Ground Cinnamon

1/3 cup Earth Balance Coconut Spread or non dairy melted butter or ghee

1 tablespoon pectin or Xanthum Gum

¼ cup coconut sugar

Directions

In a small bowl, combine vinegar with almond milk to create a buttermilk alternative. Set aside.

In another bowl, mix dry ingredients and then and pectin and keep aside.

Melt coconut oil or any butter and keep aside.

In a large bowl, add buttermilk (that we made just now), eggs, vanilla, honey and melted oil or butter and mix well and pour into the dry ingredients mix and combine well.

Cover the batter rest in the refrigerator until firm to roll out.

Preheat the oven to 350F. Grease the baking dish with parchment paper and some cooking oil.

In a piece of parchment paper about 20 inches long and dust with arrowroot powder. Dust the rolling pin with arrowroot powder also.

Roll out the dough to approximately 17 inches long and 20 inches wide. . Spread the melted butter over the rolled out dough.

Mix the filling in a bowl and spread evenly on the dough and butter.

Start rolling the dough and make about 5 rotations. Once you reach the end, pinch the ends and seal it properly.

 Cut the log into half and then again into several halves, so that you get about 16 rolls, each about 1 ½ inches thick.

Place the rolls in the baking dish and press slightly. Bake for 25 minutes until golden brown and serve hot.

Zucchini Muffins

Preparation time: 10 minutes

Cooking Time: 15 minutes

Servings: 12

Ingredients

Chia or flax seed soaked in 6 tablespoons of water for about 15 minutes

2 cups almond flour or meal

½ teaspoon baking soda

1 heaped up of grated zucchini

½ teaspoon sea salt

1 teaspoon ground cinnamon

Splash of unsweetened almond milk

1/3 cup of coconut oil melted

Directions

Preheat the oven to 425F and grease the muffin tray with coconut oil.

Cu the ends of the zucchini and grate them.

In a large bowl, add almond flour, baking soda, salt, cinnamon, grated zucchini and mix well.

Add chia or flax seeds, a splash of almond milk, coconut oil and mix to get a moist batter.

Fill in the muffin tray and bake for 15 minutes and enjoy warm with some almond butter or avocado.

Sweet Potato Biscuits

Preparation time: 10 minutes

Cooking Time: 17 minutes

Servings: 8-10 biscuits

Ingredients

1 cup gluten free all purpose flour

½ cup coconut flour

2 teaspoons baking powder

½ teaspoon salt

1 teaspoon baking soda

2/3 cup white sweet potato cooked and skin removed

4 tablespoons coconut oil (chilled)

2 eggs

½ cup dairy free buttermilk (1/2 cup coconut milk mixed with 1 tablespoon lemon juice)

1 tablespoon honey

Additional flour for dusting

Directions

Preheat the oven to 400 F. Line the baking tray with parchment paper.

In a mixing bowl, add gluten free flour, coconut flour, salt, baking soda and baking powder. Add coconut oil and mix well with the dry ingredients until it looks like coarse crumbs.

In a food processor and add sweet potato and eggs, puree until smooth. Add coconut milk, honey and puree until well blended.

Pour into the dry crumb mix. Mix everything gently with a spatula until combined.

Dust the work surface with some flour and place the dough on it. Pat and spread the dough gently with your hand till it is about 1 ½ inch thick.

Use a biscuit cutter and cut out biscuits and place them on the baking tray. Bake for 17 minutes until light golden brown and serve with some honey.

Butternut Cookie Biscuits

Preparation time: 10 minutes

Cooking Time: 15 minutes

Servings: 24 cookies

Ingredients

¼ teaspoon gluten free baking powder

1 cup coconut flour

1 ½ teaspoons granulated stevia

7 ounces cashew butter

Pinch sea salt

4 eggs beaten slightly

2 tablespoons coconut oil

2 ½ teaspoons natural vanilla extract

2 tablespoons coconut milk

Directions

Preheat the oven to 350F and grease a baking tray.

In a large bowl; add baking powder, coconut flour, stevia and salt. Heat the cashew butter a bit and combine with the eggs, coconut oil, vanilla and coconut milk well.

Add the dry ingredients and make dough. Roll the dough out at 8 mm thickness. Cut out biscuits and place on the tray.

Bake for 25 minutes until golden and crisp to bite. Leave to cool and dust with stevia if needed.

Sponge Cake with Vanilla Cream

Preparation time: 15 minutes

Cooking Time: 10 minutes

Servings: 8-10 slices

Ingredients

Sponge cake

3 large sized eggs

3 tablespoons xylitol

1 teaspoon of homemade vanilla extract

3 tablespoons of almond flour or finely ground almonds

3 tablespoons of rice flour (brown of white flour will do)

Pinch of salt

Vanilla Cream

1 ¼ cup of rice milk

2 tablespoons coconut oil

2 tablespoons tapioca starch/manioc

½ teaspoon stevia powder

1 tablespoon of vanilla extract

Topping

2 cups of red berries that you prefer

Directions

Preheat the oven to 320F and line the baking sheet with some coconut oil and sprinkle rice flour and keep aside.

To prepare the sponge cake, separate the egg yolks and whites and whisk the yolks with vanilla extract and xylitol until frothy and creamy. Add a pinch of salt to egg whites and beat until frothy and it should not slip down the dish.

In a bowl mix the almond and rice flours.

Gently add the egg whites over the egg yolks and then pour the flour mix over this and whisk until everything gets well combined.

Pour the mixed dough into the tin, smooth the batter and place in the oven. Bake for 20 minutes and check if cooked. A needle should be clean and dry when inserted and pulled out of the cooked cake. Leave the cake in the oven for 10 minutes and do not open the door or it will sink.

Prepare the vanilla cream by melting the coconut oil in a saucepan and then pour 100ml of rice milk over it. Leave it to boil at medium heat.

Mix in stevia, tapioca starch and vanilla seeds into the remaining rice milk, and combine well.

Once the rice milk begins hot and not yet boiled, add the cool rice milk and stir until smooth, and the milk should boil and become thick and creamy. Leave to cool the cream.

Set the cake on the plate and top the cake with the cream and layer fruit of you choice and enjoy.

Hazelnut Loaf Cake

Preparation time: 15 minutes

Cooking Time: 15 minutes

Servings: 12 slices

Ingredients

1 cup dates, soaked and pitted

4 eggs of size 6

¼ cup virgin coconut oil, liquid

1 cup flax seed grounds

1 ½ teaspoon baking powder

1 ¼ cup coarsely ground hazelnut

2 tablespoons shredded coconut to decorate

5 tablespoons goji berries, optional

Directions

Preheat the oven to 350 F.

Soak the dates in warm water for about 20 minutes, then drain and grind to a paste, but it should not be superfine.

Melt the coconut oil and keep aside.

In a bowl, mix liquid coconut oil, eggs, dates and baking powder. In another bowl, mix ground hazelnut and linseed well.

Add the ground nut mix to the egg mix and form dense dough and incorporate about 15 grams of goji berries. Pour the cake dough into a prepared pan and bake for 35 minutes.

Decorate with shredded coconut and goji berries and enjoy.

Chocolate Cashew Cake

Preparation time: 10 minutes

Cooking Time: 15 minutes

Servings: 12-15 slices

Ingredients

Cashew Cream

½ cup water

¾ cup cashews

1 teaspoon lemon juice

Pinch of salt

¼ teaspoon apple cider vinegar

Cake -dry ingredients

1-2/3 gluten free flour mix

½ cup ground walnuts

1 teaspoon baking soda

½ cup cocoa powder

½ teaspoon salt

Cake-wet ingredients

½ cup agave

½ cup vegetable oil

½ cup cashew cream (from above)

½ cup maple flavored agave

Vegetable spray for pan

½ cup water

Frosting ingredients

¼ cup agave

¾ cup margarine

½ cup cocoa powder

¼ cup maple flavored agave

1 teaspoon vanilla

½ cup unflavored soy or almond milk

Garnish-½ cup chopped walnuts

Directions

For cashew cream-Soak cashews in water for 3-4 Minutes, cover the bowl and keep aside. Once soft, rinse well, and place the cashews in a blender with lemon juice, water, apple cider vinegar and some salt. Blend until smooth, thick and creamy.

For the cake-preheat the oven to 350F and spray a baking pan with vegetable oil.

Take the food processor, add walnuts, and pulse until they are ground completely and but not to a paste form. Next add, gluten flour, baking soda, and cocoa powder, salt and pulse well again until everything is well mixed.

In another bowl, add vegetable oil, maple agave, agave, and cashew cream and mix well with ½ cup water.

Mix the wet and dry ingredients and combine well and then pour into the prepared baking pan.

Bake for 35 minutes until the center of the cake springs back when touched. Leave to cool on a rack.

For frosting and garnish - in a stand-up mixer and mix the frosting ingredients and beat until creamy and fluffy. Cool in the fridge.

Chop walnuts and set aside.

Once the cake has cooled, place on a platter and frost the cake and sprinkle walnuts and enjoy.

Chocolate Banana Cake

Preparation time: 10 minutes

Cooking Time: 15 minutes

Servings: 6-8 slices

Ingredients

Dry Ingredients

1/3 cup coconut flour

2/3cup almond flour

2/3cup arrowroot starch

½ teaspoon baking powder

½ cup cocoa powder

1 ½ teaspoon baking soda

½ teaspoon cinnamon

½ teaspoon salt

Wet Ingredients

¼ cup chocolate almond milk

¼ cup + 4 tablespoons rice milk

¼ cup coconut oil

2 tablespoon ground flax seed

½ cup honey

2 teaspoons apple cider vinegar

1 packet unflavored gelatin (vegan)

1 over ripe banana mashed

1 teaspoon evaporated coffee crystals or espresso powder

Directions

Melt coconut oil and agave or honey in the microwave and mix well. Mix wet ingredients in a bowl and add flax and gelatin and let them soak in the liquids. Blend them well.

Sift the dry ingredients in another bowl. Then add the wet ingredients to them and mix well.

Pour the batter in a baking pan and place the pan in a preheated oven at 350F at 25 minutes. Once cooked, let it cool for half an Minute and then slice and serve.

Chocolate Chip Cheesecake-Filled Cupcakes

Preparation time: 10 minutes

Cooking Time: 10 minutes

Servings: 3 dozen cupcakes

Ingredients

Cake

½ cup arrowroot starch

4 cups gluten free flour mix

1 teaspoon unflavored gelatin (vegan)

1 ½ cups cocoa

1 tablespoon baking soda

2 2/3 cups sugar substitute such as xylitol

1 tablespoon baking powder

3 ½ cups almond milk

2 teaspoons vanilla

4 scoops stevia extract

½ cup melted coconut oil

¼ cup apple cider vinegar

Filling

3 tablespoons water

3 cups nuts or seeds

3/8 cup lemon juice

3/16 teaspoon salt

4 teaspoon vanilla extract

1 cup chocolate chips (sugar free variety)

6 scoops stevia extract

Directions

Prepare the filling first and leave to cool. So first, place all the filling ingredients into a powerful blender and blend until smooth and creamy.

Fold in chocolate chips into the cheesecake mix and stir and keep aside.

To prepare the cake batter, first mix the dry ingredients in a large bowl.

In another bowl, mix the wet ingredients in another bowl and pour into the dry ingredients and mix well.

Pour the batter into prepared muffin tins. Fill the tins only until it is half full.

Then gently pour 2 teaspoons of cheesecake mix and then cover with the rest of the cake batter.

Bake for 30 minutes in a preheated oven at 350F and enjoy warm or cold.

Carrot Cake

Preparation time: 10 minutes

Cooking Time: 10 minutes

Servings: 12

Ingredients

Cake

2 slices of pineapple

3 carrots

1 banana

1 cup of pecans

2 cups of almonds

½ cup almond milk

1 cup buckwheat flour

½ cup maple syrup

½ cup raisins

½ cup dates

1 tablespoon cinnamon powder

3 tablespoons of chia seeds

Icing

1 avocado

1 ripe banana

3 tablespoons of maple syrup

1 tablespoon of coconut oil

6 medjool dates

1 tablespoon of nut butter

A handful of pecans for sprinkling on top

1 heaped teaspoon of cinnamon

Directions

Preheat the oven to 350°F.

In a food processor, place the pecans and pulse until coarsely ground. It is fine to have a few pieces to crunch later on. Grind the almonds to form fine flour.

Grate the carrots and keep aside. In a large bowl; add buckwheat flour, grated carrots, almond flour, pineapple, banana, almond milk, chia seeds, maple syrup, cinnamon and dates and mix well to get a sticky mixture.

Grease a baking pan with coconut oil. Pour batter into a baking pan and finally add in coarsely pecan pieces and raisins on top. Bake until golden brown for 30 minutes and leave to cool.

For the icing, place all the icing ingredients in the processor and pulse to get a creamy caramel colored frosting. Spread over the cooled cake and finally sprinkle some pecan pieces and slice and enjoy.

Terrific Tiramisu

Preparation time: 10 minutes

Cooking Time: 15 minutes

Servings: 8-12

Ingredients

Sponge Cake

2 cup coconut sugar

8 large eggs, separated

½ cup + 2 tablespoons boiling water

2 teaspoon vanilla

2 cups gluten free flour, sifted

¼ teaspoon salt

Additional Ingredients

12 ounces non-dairy cream cheese

1 ½ cups coconut cream or full fat coconut milk

1 ¼ cups powdered coconut sugar (1 1/8 cup coconut sugar with 4 teaspoons arrowroot powder ground in coffee grinder)

1 ¼ teaspoons vanilla

⅜ cup chocolate liqueur

⅜ cup espresso

⅜ cup marsala wine (optional)

3 ounces bittersweet chocolate, grated or finely chopped

3 tablespoons pure Dutch processed cocoa or unsweetened cocoa powder

Directions

Sponge Cake

Preheat the oven to 350F. Grease three 8-inch cake pans. Line bottoms with parchment paper and then grease parchment paper.

In a mixer, beat yolks and sugar on high for 3-4 minutes. Scape sides of bowl as needed.

Pour hot water slowly while mixer is on high speed.

Allow to cool of a couple of minutes and then blend in the vanilla.

Add flour. Mix at low speed until smooth.

In a separate bowl, beat egg whites to firm stiff peaks.

Gently fold in half the egg whites to the cake batter until just mixed. Then fold in the other half to the egg whites until just mixed. Care must be taken to over fold and deflate the eggs too much.

Pour batter evenly into cake pans.

Bake for about 25 minutes. The cake should spring back when pressed with your finger. When done, allow to cool 10 minutes.

Invert pans to remove cakes.

Filling and assembly

In a mixing bowl, beat together the cream cheese, coconut cream, powdered sugar and vanilla on high until stiff peaks form. Add chocolate liqueur while mixer is running until blended. (Some people have suggested doubling the amount of cream mixture – this is a personal preference.)

If using Marsala wine, combine with espresso. Brush espresso or combination over all three cake layers

Evenly spoon ¼ of the cream mixture over the first cake layer. Sprinkle with ½ of the chocolate. Top with second cake, spread with ¼ of the cream mixture.

Add the third cake layer. Spread both the top and sides with the remaining cream mixture.

Refrigerate at least 8 Minutes. Dust the top with the cocoa.

Vanilla Almond Cake

Preparation time: 10 minutes

Cooking Time: 15 minutes

Servings: 6-8

Ingredients

Cake

⅓ cup coconut flour

2 cups almond flour

½ cup almond milk

3 eggs

½ cup olive oil

2 teaspoons vanilla paste or vanilla extract

½ cup coconut sugar

½ teaspoon baking soda

1 teaspoon baking powder

Topping

2 tablespoons maple syrup

15 ounces canned coconut cream

1-pound unsweetened shredded coconut

1 cup fresh mixed berries

Directions

Preheat the oven to 350F. Grease a baking tin and line with parchment paper.

In a mixing bowl, add milk, eggs, oil, sugar, vanilla paste and whisk until well combined. Add baking soda, flour and baking powder and mix thoroughly.

Pour the batter into the baking tin and bake for 45 minutes and check whether the cake tester comes out clean. Leave the cake to cool for 30 minutes.

Meanwhile, make the topping. In a mixing bowl, add coconut cream and maple syrup and mix well. Freeze a bit for 10 minutes so that the cream hardens a bit. Once it ready to apply over the cake, spread gently over the cake, and top with mixed berries. Store in fridge until ready to serve.

Blueberry Lemon Cake

Preparation time: 10 minutes

Cooking Time: 15 minutes

Servings: 6-8

Ingredients

Dry Ingredients

¼ teaspoon sea salt

2/3 cup coconut flour

Wet Ingredients

1 cup coconut milk

½ cup coconut oil

1 tablespoon lemon juice

6 eggs

1 tablespoon lemon zest

1 tablespoon vanilla extract

1 cup fresh blueberries

2-3 drops of vanilla liquid stevia

Directions

Preheat the oven to 350F and grease the cake pan and keep aside.

Take the food processor, add eggs and pulse properly until it is whipped. Then add coconut milk along with 2 drops of liquid vanilla stevia, lemon zest and lemon juice. Pulse until mixed well.

Next, add ¼ cup of butter and ¼ cup of virgin coconut oil (or add ½ cup of virgin coconut oil) and mix well.

Then add the dry ingredients and mix gently. Check the sweetness and add more if you like. Pour into cake tin and finally add the fresh blueberries and stir the batter.

Bake for 40 minutes until cooked well. Enjoy warm.

Orange Almond Cake

Preparation time: 10 minutes

Cooking Time: 10 minutes

Servings: 12

Cake

1 cup almond meal

2 large navel oranges

1 cup coconut sugar

6 large eggs

1 teaspoon baking powder

Glaze

2 tablespoons water

¾ cup apricot jam

Blanched almonds or almond flakes

Directions

In a large pot and place the oranges in it and boil in simmering heat for 2 Minutesuntil very soft. Then drain and leave to cool. Once it is cool, chop, remove seeds and puree the skin and flesh in a food processor.

Preheat the oven to 170C and grease a baking pan and line with baking paper. Dust with almond flour and keep aside.

In a bowl, put in sugar, almond meal, baking powder and whisk. In another bowl, whisk eggs until fluffy. Add the orange puree and almond mix to the eggs and stir gently.

Pour into the cake tins and bake for 1 Minute. Leave to cool once well cooked and then place on a plate.

Meanwhile, make the cake glaze by boiling jam with 2 tablespoons of water for 5 minutes. Stir and boil till it gets syrupy. Pour into a bowl through a sieve and keep aside.

Pour over the cooled cake and serve warm or cold.

Delicious Kale Smoothie

Preparation time: 5 min

Servings: 2

Ingredients:

2-3 ice cubes

1½ cup apple juice

3-4 kale leaves

1 apple, cut

1 cup strawberries

½ tsp cloves

Directions:

Combine ingredients in blender and purée until smooth.

Cherry Smoothie

Preparation time: 5 min

Servings: 2

Ingredients:

2-3 ice cubes

1½ cup almond or coconut milk

1½ cup pitted and frozen cherries

½ avocado

1 tsp cinnamon

1 tsp chia seeds

Directions

Combine all ingredients into a blender and process until smooth.
Enjoy!

Banana and Coconut Smoothie

Preparation time: 5 min

Servings: 2

Ingredients:

1 frozen banana, chopped

1½ cup coconut water

2-3 small broccoli florets

1 tbsp coconut butter

Directions

Add all ingredients into a blender and blend until the smoothie turns into an even and smooth consistency. Enjoy!

Avocado and Pineapple Smoothie

Preparation time: 5 min

Servings: 2

Ingredients:

3-4 ice cubes

1½ cup coconut water

½ avocado

2 cups diced pineapple

Directions:

Combine all ingredients in a blender, and blend until smooth. Enjoy!

Vanilla Macadamia Ice cream

Preparation time: 4-6 Minutes

Cooking Time: 0 minutes

Servings: 2 ½ cups

Ingredients

½ cup raw macadamia nuts

1 can about 13.5 ounces full fat coconut milk

½ cup Medjool dates pitted

1 tablespoon vanilla extract

1 tablespoon honey or grade B maple syrup

1 vanilla bean

Directions

Place all ingredients in a blender and blend until smooth and creamy.

Transfer to a airtight container and freeze for 4-6 Minutes or pour into an ice cream maker and make ice cream as per Directions.

You can serve with the bananas foster topping from the previous recipe.

Fudgesicles

Preparation time: 2-4 Minutes

Cooking Time: 0 minutes

Servings: 6-8

Ingredients

1 cup almond milk

1 can full fat coconut milk

3 tablespoons cocoa

¼ teaspoon stevia (or 1-3 tablespoons coconut nectar, honey, maple syrup)

1 teaspoon vanilla

Directions

Blend everything until smooth.

Pour into fudgesicle molds and freeze until frozen.

Almond Chocolate Mousse

Preparation time: 10 minutes

Cooking Time: 45 minutes

Servings: 6-8

Ingredients

2 tablespoons agave nectar

½ cup raw natural almonds and water to cover them

Pinch of fine sea salt

½ - 1 cup vanilla or plain or unsweetened almond milk

1 ounce of good quality chocolate chopped

10-20 drops vanilla stevia liquid to taste

Directions

Soak almonds in water for 12 Minutes, remove the skins and then blend the almonds with glycerin and salt and keep aside.

In a medium heat proof bowl and place chocolate in it. Boil almond milk and pour into the chocolate. Leave untouched for 30-40 seconds and the chocolate will melt.

Pour the chocolate almond mix along with the previously blended almond mix and blend on high to get a creamy mousse mix. Taste and add more stevia if needed. Pour into small bowls and refrigerate until ready to serve and it should be a bit firm.

Strawberry Lime Granita

Preparation time: 5-6 Minutes

Cooking Time: 0 minutes

Servings: 4-6

Ingredients

6 tablespoons fresh lime juice

1 pound fresh strawberries hulled

½ cup water

1/3 cup agave nectar

Directions

Place all ingredients in a food processor and blend well.

Pour the mix into a container and freeze well. Then scrape it with a fork to make the granita.

Pile into serving bowls and enjoy.

Strawberry Ice Cream Bars

Preparation time: 4-6 Minutes

Cooking Time: 0 minutes

Servings: 2-4

Ingredients

1 ½ cups of fresh or frozen strawberries

2 cups of coconut cream

¼ cup honey

Directions

Blend all the ingredients in a blender until there are no lumps and it is creamy.

Pour into Popsicle molds, freeze and enjoy later.

Carrot and Mango Smoothie

Preparation time: 5 min

Servings: 2

Ingredients:

1 cup frozen mango chunks

1 cup carrot juice

½ cup orange juice

1 carrot, chopped

1 tsp chia seeds

1 tsp grated ginger

Directions:

Combine all ingredients in a blender, and blend until smooth. Enjoy!

Strawberry and Coconut Smoothie

Preparation time: 5 min

Servings: 2

Ingredients:

3-4 ice cubes

1½ cup coconut milk

2 cups fresh strawberries

1 tsp chia seeds

Directions:

Place all ingredients in a blender and purée until smooth. Enjoy!

Beautiful Skin Smoothie

Preparation time: 5 min

Servings: 2

Ingredients:

1 cup frozen strawberries

1½ cup green tea

1 peach, chopped

½ avocado

5-6 raw almonds

1 tsp coconut oil

Directions:

Place all ingredients in a blender and purée until smooth. Enjoy!

Conclusion

L iving gluten-free can be overwhelming when it comes to food preparation. Using your slow cooker makes it so much easier. You get great tasting food, one pot meal, and an easy clean up!.

So there you have it, the simplest way to live gluten-free with these easy to prepare and stress-free one pot meals your family will love. I hope you found several to add to your go-to recipes Thank you so much for downloading and reading my book.

This e-book can save you with the hassle of doing a month-long meal prepping with its delicious and simple recipes. The recipes are pretty simple and easy to stick to your gluten-free diet. And, they deliver overall fantastic health benefits. You can even swap ingredients with your favorite ones and experiment with the recipes to make your meal plan that you will look forward to eating all month long.

Through this book you have learned what gluten is, why it may be bad for you, and what it does to your body if you are sensitive to it. You have also learned how important it is to start the Gluten Free Diet as soon as you have found out that you have gluten sensitivity or intolerance. This book has also shown to you the steps to take to get started on the Gluten Free Diet and which foods you should choose and which to avoid. You have also acquired a variety of breakfast, main dish, and side dish recipes that will help you get started on the diet.

Now, you only have to collect more recipes and build healthy habits that will help you follow the Gluten Free Diet easily, sustainably, and enjoyably. It may be difficult at times, but never give up on your health! All efforts are worth it when you have a body that is strong, healthy, and full of energy. It is, after all, the most priceless asset you have.

Lightning Source UK Ltd.
Milton Keynes UK
UKHW020827180321
380564UK00005B/46